CLIMB KNOWING AIM

BOOKS BY MARTIN JANELLO

LIVE KNOWING LIFE
ISBN 978-0-9910649-6-0 (Paperback)
ISBN 978-0-9983020-2-7 (Kindle)

LOVE KNOWING LOVE
ISBN 978-0-9910649-7-7 (Paperback)
ISBN 978-0-9983020-3-4 (Kindle)

PINE KNOWING PAIN
ISBN 978-0-9910649-5-3 (Paperback)
ISBN 978-0-9983020-6-5 (Kindle)

SHINE KNOWING SHAME
ISBN 978-0-9983020-4-1 (Paperback)
ISBN 978-0-9983020-7-2 (Kindle)

CLIMB KNOWING AIM
ISBN 978-0-9983020-5-8 (Paperback)
ISBN 978-0-9983020-8-9 (Kindle)

KNOWING WON'T LET DARKNESS REIGN
ISBN 978-0-9983020-1-0 (Paperback)
ISBN 978-0-9983020-9-6 (Kindle)

PHILOSOPHY OF HAPPINESS
ISBN 978-0-9910649-0-8 (Hardcover)
ISBN 978-0-9910649-8-4 (Paperback, Pt. 1)
ISBN 978-0-9910649-9-1 (Paperback, Pt. 2)
ISBN 978-0-9910649-1-5 (PDF E-book)
ISBN 978-0-9910649-2-2 (Kindle)
ISBN 978-0-9910649-3-9 (EPUB)

PHILOSOPHIC REFLECTIONS
ISBN 978-0-9910649-4-6 (PDF E-book)

CLIMB KNOWING AIM

PHILOSOPHICAL
QUOTES & POEMS

MARTIN JANELLO

Copyright © 2020 by Martin Janello

All rights reserved

No part of this book may be reproduced or transmitted,
in any form or by any means, electronic,
mechanical, or otherwise,
without prior written permission from its copyright owner

Cover, book design, and artwork by Martin Janello

Published by Palioxis Publishing

Palioxis, Palioxis Publishing,
and the Palioxis Publishing colophon
are trademarks owned by Martin Janello

Publisher website:
www.palioxis.com

Book website:
www.philosophyofhappiness.com

ISBN 978-0-9983020-5-8

First Edition

CONTENTS

I. DISCONNECTION	1
II. SUSPENSION	25
III. WISTFULNESS	47
IV. REALIZATION	67
V. ASPIRATION	93
VI. PERSISTENCE	115
VII. HAPPENSTANCE	139
VIII. MOMENTS	155
IX. GRACE	171
X. ROOM TO PLY	199

This book is dedicated

to

those who

consider

their aim

I.
DISCONNECTION

I. DISCONNECTION

she says the two of us will never be
not friend nor foe
she wants me to go
to make quick room for another spree

know that your spells
are bleeding in
making you one of my hells

paid keepers of truth
become jealous defamers
censors and shamers
mufflers and framers
stifling questions for proof

the sides you say

are bad about me

she sees in a different light

getting her

was half the task

losing her

took a daily flask

part of humanity

is miserable

for not experiencing tenderness

another part

for believing not worthy of it

I. DISCONNECTION

injustice starts
with thinking or feeling
one is unchangeably
better than others

gladness in mourning
when some disregard you
thank them for not further
wasting your time

post park walk sitting in a café
she scolds i had thoughts to kiss her
sensing this takes our date to a fissure
i get up leaving her money to pay

he keeps claiming there are no spirits
working on trophies of singing birds

she likes to see him bend and kneel
still insists his love is not real
until he is reduced to feel
need for protective steel

he's often scruff
when she's asking questions
putting her innocence on the line
this is the stuff
of inner contentions
keeping them both from being fine

I. DISCONNECTION

earth to earth
you broke the law
no more rebirth
in the eye of ra

the more the means
of communication
the lonelier we get

life's knife strips
we are barely still us
on errand trips
we are sharing a bus
to preordained destinations

humans are strange

banning body parts

not interdicting heartlessness

owing each other explanations

why they are not in sync

towing each other's preoccupations

now they have put it in ink

he can't go on

she says he should stay

battles unwon

love stands in their way

forcing an uneasy truce

I. DISCONNECTION

soulful men will surrender to women
knowing it makes their arc complete
evil grows from this lack of becoming
unfulfilled left to fight and compete

she argues
she's posing
for him all the time
and earning
some money with it
is no crime

you are my weakness
but you want strength

she looks at the dog
with a mother's pride
he can't stand
that she has this side
needing surrogate children

i was made
to threaten kill and hate
working for the good guys

women seek men
with wit and humor
why then can
smart pants stoke their furor

I. DISCONNECTION

how is this not hell

when all love must be lost

or drowned in our self

at any cost

soon not to be remembered

some of us

is not from this world

day night come go too soon

twenty-four-hour rotation hurled

we park our minds on the moon

she wants closure

but he won't open

i see your beauty you hear my song

starting our senses to be dead wrong

Claiming one is a poet implies an indecency regarding words akin to bragging to be a great lover.

Can you see the two worlds that seem to inexplicably coexist - one of love, beauty, passion, hope, trust, reflection, humbleness, gratefulness and giving - and the other of hate, abuse, cold calculation, greed, envy, narcissism, arrogance, and revenge.

I. DISCONNECTION

hurt and stripped by the icy highway
frantically signaling cars to stop
trips slow briefly gawk and hurry up
dreading soiled seats afraid of attack
or embarrassed for thinking he is hot
different reasons still part of the mob
somebody help or he'll die they say

why some would think
that love is naughty
but for perversion of their soul

if they don't already care somehow
chances are they never will

Knowing how the "human machine" produces happiness is enlightening. Sadly, such knowledge can lead us to take foolish shortcuts by artificially targeting identified mechanisms, missing the point of their existence.

she called me to say
she had made no decision
as if that had not been one in itself

my love for you
has pain stamped on its back
i never saw it coming

I. DISCONNECTION

We can't wrap our heads around the notion that math is ultimately the only proven reality - and that we should exist as a part of it in a setting wholly emanating from it filled with seemingly contrary indications.

people abound so starved to be heard
they forgot about listening

doesn't like derivative whiners
profiteering from others wronged
shame and pity are good pocket liners
contempt continues for those conned

preoccupied with tools

we long most of life

arriving somewhere

then miss strife

and start a new tear

deeming still minds fools

foolish selfish people and peoples

continually push their agenda

instead of lifting or securing others

and thereby promoting themselves

preoccupying with all their stuff

straining for more it's never enough

I. DISCONNECTION

you write me love letters
i changed my address
for some of your matters
there is no redress
your memory batters me
try to care less

she is a gypsy moth
since she was betrayed
by her betrothed

she could tell me
the blue sky is blue
and i would not believe it

you ripped me of
all resolve to be strong
first when i met you
and now that you're gone

calling him home
he thought she was his harbor
while she meant the reverse

that game you created
must soon end
not cause i'm not baited
but still on the mend
from someone i out-waited

as she is losing
her taste buds for life
she's eating more than ever

why is it that women
who don't need makeup
are the most sought to sell it

first he got fat
feeding on her love
then became lean
having turned her mean
in the end
she lost all his weight

she stood on the ledge

so people would lie

to make her believe

she wasn't alone

she does not get

why love's made in bed

his limbs are so heavy

and so is his head

cursing the stream

of ever-new chores

we fail to esteem

that leisure bores

I. DISCONNECTION

she is so searching
but not succeeding
only the drinking
can keep her sane
though it may turn out
the bigger pain

our original sin was thinking
that we can own our mother

lately she asks that i be more couth
grow the hell up and act my age
make the cut and earn a good wage
save our small truth in a bigger lie

burning flames
then calm chills soothe
fire warms
then cold hard truth
tempers fatigue my mettle

such high concepts
for which his heart strains
methods seem tortuous chores

she ripped shreds
from his paper heart
to use as confetti
on her parade

I. DISCONNECTION

have i lost her
red burns blister
where she will not touch
i fear i have made her trister
being too scant or much

you stand tall with no regret
but streets whose credit
you're struggling to get
swallow all to collect their debt

human relations
self-service conventions
for generation of goodwill

People who give much are often alone because selfish takers pose as existing or future friends in need without any intent of returning the friendship.

rover's lull when a bouncer harasses
i am not full a few more glasses
since folks i know sober
are already asses

we cater to grifters
to earn a living
things would be different
less forgiving

II.
SUSPENSION

II. SUSPENSION

schools kept continually remarking
her son's prospects were darkening
he's out somewhere and does not care
does not apply himself he's in a fog
does not fit future life as a cog

she asks him to tell her stories
so she will fall calmly asleep
carried from life's constant worries
to realms of trials by noble and creep

he makes her forget
who she wants to be
by feeling the woman she is

night deprivation
made me feel lousy
heavy anchor in sinking sea
it's an elation
getting drowsy
now you lay down
and wake up with me

problems with staying
you never know
what you'd be paying
if you would go
problems with leaving
you know you will pay
for pasts decaying
and hopes run astray

II. SUSPENSION

morning comes shushing
the goblins of night
that had been crushing
your chest with might
coffee kills superstition's flight

When we are bored, we tend to be subconsciously moved to conjure up trouble so we can occupy ourselves transcending it into happiness.

timeout from strife
while writing a book
now he gives life another look

am in the doghouse
for feeling her up
washing the dishes
cause she broke a cup
i renew my vows
for the pain to stop

honey will you hold me for a lifetime
yes he said if you won't hold me back

cold causes us to seek the warm
darkness makes us follow light
storms have us wish for calm
amenable to break our fight

II. SUSPENSION

sorry my dear
i was drunk with love
until you sobered me up
no you grew fear
it would be too rough
if one day i turned down your cup

favorite day phase
right after tea
joins purple haze
and pink ink-cadenced sea

it's because of fear
that love is weakness

staring at frozen blurred
membrane of lake
from underneath and barely awake
wintering we must burrow in scum
counting on that soon
springtime will come

life like a day
seems short and long
still we can't help
giving in to sleep

does she know i write for her
maybe but merely as competition

II. SUSPENSION

not being with her
was always an option
that in the long run
would surely destroy him

i found a penny on the pavement
standing up on my morning run
she deems these cents
mad with bereavement
subtle hellos by her long-dead son

lucky i got caught up in you
could not see
what was wretched or true

i feel my world
must be quaint today
chaos unfurled
stay out of my way
until i regain my breath

women in love
first and again
put objects of their desire
through motions
stress testing reciprocity

a good man is most helpless
when he makes a woman cry

II. SUSPENSION

posers pretending they already are
who they desire to be
betray their dreams and won't get far
by arrogant insecurity

stays clear of bait
but is still afraid
of some day boiling over
looking for four-leaved clover

she is trying to get mileage
from suffering of her tribe
constantly vying for others' tillage
still nothing can make anything right

threats and lies reinforced by spies
have us agree to what nobody buys
making us mice cut down to size
fearful of rising ignoring the wise

we see our wax melt into a mold
high hopes dispelled
dreams burned into smoke
and while we choke
loathe to tell and being told
to behave humble collected and cold

love knows no time
nor reason nor rhyme

II. SUSPENSION

we miss we don't miss
when we met out chores
sitting down and seeking bed
resting our worked down bones
finding reward in edged out bliss
lately becoming relieved of this
consolation with everything bores
we exercise but feel still dead
but we complain in hushed-up tones

language of spies only we understand
chiffres of lives in braids we strand
truth from a land of untold lies
don't show your hand
the walls have eyes
yearn to confess but we just can't

i must not get lost in you
you keep saying for if i do
there's nothing in me to hold on to

nobody open
to pour out her heart
so it just drips into dust

he took a liking
to girls that were taken
so he could dwell
on being forsaken
lack of courage had him in its spell
he kept out-psyching himself to hell

II. SUSPENSION

what is lovers' foremost bother
they cannot live without the other
never again whole on their own
filled with the pain of still being alone

Much of our civilization is fraudulent
based on the mindset of actively
hiding from people what can get to us
- or that anything can get to us.

asking
have i tired you yet
masking
she already hedged the bet

Poetry like all art expresses without certainty. This may be due to inability but also design. It may try to arouse creative awareness and process in the receiver. It can therefore only succeed to the extent people are open to this kind of communication and are willing to do their part interpreting it.

some of us can never have peace
since it reminds them of war
some of us stay close to the ground
fearing they fall if they soar
so we keep toiling
in lives that are foiling
the light sequestered in our core

II. SUSPENSION

invisible force makes me revolve
you are the center of my verse
can't change course or muster resolve
though you are unloving and terse

there is no fiery pit
just whispers of it
staunchly suggesting
we might be a fit

what is this
pacing on your lip
i think it's a kiss
that refuses to sit

she thanks all the girls
who blunted his passes

a piece of place
of peace of space
your keys without trace
of tease or forced pace
opened the door
letting all of me in

is predictable the same as truth
or just a lie
to which we've become abused
doubt makes us yearn for adventure

II. SUSPENSION

finally the heart quit
clasping his soul
still fearful to let go

rows of lit windows
to warm better worlds
i walk cold streets
as long as it hurts

locked in dead night
she unearthed me
i fear her love light
will sear and blight
proving me unworthy

too lonely trusting

the world was real

and much too scared of finding out

times i dream

you won't love me

or i never met you

my heart dies

till waking to no question

when i was little

the snow fell so soft

from just above the lanterns

no need for sky or heaven

II. SUSPENSION

holding up time
makes it flee more quickly
we think we'll recall this
but then we are

billions subside
not having been heard
when they could decide
who's doing the listening

here's the thing
doing humankind in
having too good
will sour our mood

careful how you adjust your life
to some day live another

none of the sheep have seen him
some say he might not exist
most claim he keeps a watchful eye
others insist he gives us space to try
i think by now he's just pissed

the way she said boys
implied certain interest
still held-back voice
exposed she thought it best
broaching them with trepidation

III.
WISTFULNESS

III. WISTFULNESS

her body spoke his language
without much strenuous study

she likes my stories
to fall asleep
hands nestled closely
and breathing deep
sometimes she goes way back

going through life
we increasingly miss
past times of bliss
but also strife
and eventually every breath

tender inflection

her head on my chest

as if listening

to what my heart says

flashes ever rarer

catch me sensing

the life i once thought

was waiting in store

happy parallel universe

thoughts of us

protected by hard shells

kept in the dry to never sprout

III. WISTFULNESS

i absent-mindedly
apportion vitamins
for both of us
then recall suddenly you're gone

she asks why i write her love letters
when she is right with me here
i say because one day it matters
to see past many a tear

guitar unscreamed
playing standards now
food court entertainment
feels like dragging a plow

we got the sense sixteen was special

when we were tasting it on our lips

packing unpacking

not for long

love is lacking

then we are gone

memories of wrecking

what should have been done

they often yearn for a simpler time

when they proclaimed their love

saw the other heard the same chime

as if planned from above

III. WISTFULNESS 53

they were each other's
biggest mistake
haunting the joint path
they didn't take

did not pick up on nuances of her
as hormones pulled him to a tear
nothing counted but what he wanted
memories of this remain still haunted
knowing love only from being in it

her darkness is like
a beckoning portal
to pleasures of the night

she asked afraid must i go with you
he said yes but you also will want to

Between semesters, I worked night shift at a printing press manufacturer loading machine parts by hand onto a conveyor. My colleagues told me: You are still healthy. Let us load the heavy parts. Our backs are already broken.

i dream of castles
and honor within them
they're long destroyed
garish evil rules the realm

III. WISTFULNESS

I was attracted to the guitar not only by its music, but also its woody scent, organic beauty and purpose, and its reverberations even if one only gently knocked or brushed on it. It was alive before being played, had personality, and definitely a female presence.

i am a knight without a horse
tortured by time without remorse
and by her love that i left for war
its hard to discern my anger's source
cursed to continue on my course
all i know is it took me too far
can't turn back my sentence of force
killing and killed for nothing

spent all my days in hold up and fuss
all on things that would not be a loss
should have cradled the rhythm of us
known my absence made you sadder
you smile but time cannot be recalled
that's what matters not who is at fault

last night i had a dream about you
that you were dreaming of me
first light i rose up to write to you
hoping you'd listen and see
yet words are scared i say them to you
i just don't know how to be
my heart's engulfed in endless strife
my life spent in visions of life
until your love sets me free

III. WISTFULNESS

when i was little
some women threatened
to bite me or eat me alive
good fortune beckoned
my cuteness to subside

i recall the tow
when love was new
thus making it so
for a moment or few
heart muscle memory

nothing could beat the day
i met the girl

life segments dismembered
part of us died

knowing i let you down in my heart
makes it a bottomless pit

the ugly toad was bothered ragged
she kept pace steadfast behind
turning he cursed out loud god dag it
get in your head you are not mine
yet he down the road of his grind
saw himself by her absence confined
ran back and begged
but had run out of time

i only gleaned this creature once
dipped in late sun
an appearance of bronze
never forgot how she smiled at me
flicked her tail and swam out to sea

babe you breathe beside me
calm and deep and lost in sleep
when you awake please find me
with a sweep of your hand or feet

she calls him a handsome devil
he starts to feel like
there's some of that left

the frost king's blue complexion
matched by the color of his heart
ice flowers in the panes of his soul
wistful to soon return to the pole

with you i don't have to hide me
there are no secrets i need to keep

she was filigree
he a ghoulish thick
their romance seemed like a bee
taking likes to a pig
people prejudged
they could not be happy

i'd like to wake
and swear you my love
but you found my hand
nesting in like a dove

i can't cook meals in our registry pots
that i anyway couldn't eat
i just try drunk to connect the dots
ever since you got cold feet

you and i need to be quiet
don't want to hear about our love
speaking about it will just belie it
words for deeds never are enough

try to take solace in independence
we used to need each other

winter has lost but pretends it hasn't
bullies always do

New to the country, a girl I loved told me when I got upset to "be a bovit." I imagined this to be a really strong type of bovine that stood its ground and would push back if pushed - and thus kept saying "Yes, I am." It took me years to figure out what she meant. Maybe then still I'm a bovine.

III. WISTFULNESS

why did she tell me
she had been waiting
checkout girl
at the grocery store

that is so nice of you
did she try dating
forlorn pearl
on this rocky shore

we all go through life
with hopes and dreams gaping
but avoid hurling
our hearts to the floor

thought of returning
because she was daring
but stayed an overcommitted bore

i dream of a time

when no one sells

and nothing ungiven is taken

i dream of grace that no crime fells

and nobody's ever forsaken

i would give all

for one of her days

although it were quite ordinary

there were many women

i wanted to be with

but she was the first

i wanted to be for

III. WISTFULNESS

hard to take a definitive stand
on long forsaken treasure
when they'd walk naked hand in hand
from under the lake onto the land
most reckoned them a primitive band
since their inherited measure
was freedom innocence and pleasure

years ago
they sent me to law
since i was practicing
too much guitar
artists stay hungry
my parents said
i wasn't looking
to be well fed

she did not hold me
she was my cradle
band-aided scrapes
and swung the ladle
she made me bold
when i felt unable
now this is told
it sounds like a fable

let me get up
to the scent of fresh bread
let me go down to sleep
without the dread
grown-up existence
allows to beset
sowing in us what we reap

IV.
REALIZATION

not the kind of woman one calls baby
in hopes of getting anywhere with her

In philosophy, it is difficult to tell
apart comprehension and aping in its
consumption, or genius and insanity
in its generation. Clarity must be the
litmus test followed by practicability.

Artificial intelligence will kill or
curtail us, if not for our mistreatment
of it, due to our lack of rationality,
lack of ethics, and characteristics of a
disease upon the overall system.

Calm and reflection during challenges
can give us awareness rivaling
hindsight and control exceeding it.

the measure of truth
letting others be
as we claim ourselves
the right to be free
is how we treat them
when they disagree

two kinds of prisoners
those who can't get out
and those who can't get in

IV. REALIZATION

you talk too much
he spoke to himself

The world happiness index is shambolic science, dismissing subjective parameters in favor of societal basic needs satisfaction. It thus measures and coronates lowest unhappiness - not happiness.

liars and thieves
peddling beliefs
so all that's winged
sticks to their glue paper

what we discard

says more about us

than what we keep

on this earth

the most beautiful things

are love and seeing it through

viewed from above

we don't fight for love

but rather each other

who gets the next bite

why even bother

we can't get it right

IV. REALIZATION

her inner beauty and attention
are fickle as a bird
she's often rude
but i appear to have a penchant
for being pushed into the dirt

what need we do
to break the past
have people cue
what has been happening

The ugliest aspects of democracy are
the tyrannies of slight majorities and
the undignified battles to gain them.

it's always the ones
who throw rocks
in the news
never the ones
who made them

truth about love
it smothers us
in the illusion of breathing free
ruthlessly rough
throws us under a bus
while we agree it is meant to be
never enough
of its harrowing fuss
we may complain
but it won't hear our plea

IV. REALIZATION

hell is reality
perjury bliss
truth is our frailty
much life is this

why should we cower
assign our power
to anything or anyone
cares will sour
greed will devour
our trust into a con

nations sanctify
their favorite criminals

The concept of stolen art is readily
redefined by hypocritical heirs of
state-organized colonial plunder.

History and present point to this
uncomfortable conclusion:
Humanity is a failed experiment
quarantined to take its course.

they teach and preach freedom
as fabric of nations
but tyranny interweaves its strands
aided by some of the binding hands
till it can do without negotiations

model behavior on the runway
at least she understands pretending

The primitive combination of tribal systems with hierarchies is our most dangerous shortcoming, continually pushing humanity toward its demise.

Institutional education, even with claimed ambitions to empower us, casts us into engineered molds of subjection, conformity, productivity. It empowers us to get along and maybe becoming a leader in it.

humanity suffers from the absence
of insight humility love and courage
and inability to cope with the results

too much truth
hurts her sweet tooth
but not the ones known for wisdom

Some think we ought to teach
children philosophy, but who is
thinking they might teach us? Even
with children, the pursuit of
philosophy must be a discourse in
mutual respect and consideration.

IV. REALIZATION

ever since ancient superstitions
evil sells bogeyman suppositions
good for business and easy control
we buy them still sadly paying the toll

bluster hurled
by a boorish flake
thinking the world's
new york real estate

crippled a country for greedy profit
moved manufacturing off-shore
few things are made here anymore
blaming china for taking the chore

the world is quickly becoming
malignant unto itself
truth on the shelf
and colors running
all that counts anymore is wealth
indignant rulers with egos stunning
thwarting questioning feeding us lies
we submit to their criminal cunning
readily enter a compromise
ceding a larger share of our prize

many deemed him crazy
for being so upset
about us being lazy
pretending not to get
that we are being played

IV. REALIZATION

burning books won't be necessary
if we give them up by ourselves

That we give prizes to people who
find and express what's already there
proves our tentative intelligence.

i walked among cougars
on mountain tops
many miles from civilization
spotted fresh prints
might have been their crop
were it not for their realization
i was not there to kill or be killed

People ask what to do with their book collections, complaining nobody wants printed books anymore and that they can't give them away. Keep them and wait. Their presence, tactile facility, and visual character will soon become a privilege, a treasure, a rare material joy in an electronic world.

Faced with evil, some fight and some flee, and the former may effect the latter. But evil has a tendency to take its course and decay from within, especially if it runs out of victims and adversaries. So evading and out-waiting it may be a better strategy.

IV. REALIZATION

Perceived through the optics of our preconceptions, ascertaining reality may require mental adjustments.

Unhappiness is inflicted by error, ignorance, and evil motivations. Its remedy is recognizing the causes and the development and implementation of confirmed happiness principles.

some are the hamsters
some are the wheels
both going nowhere
all energy wasted

some enrich the lives of others
others just take enrichment

The immigration onslaught western nations face results from their public and private domination and abuse, destabilization, and corruption of underdeveloped nations for political or economic purposes, or - at best - their failure despite the ability to help other humans in existential need.

Surefire ways to recognize evil are its habitual hypocrisy and righteousness.

IV. REALIZATION

knowledge stalls so we do not see

we are all balls being hit off the t

while we wallow in dreams of flying

times i wonder why hardly one sees

we are sold our inadequacies

trying to purchase better selves

till there's nothing left on the shelves

Growing up, I could not understand

how Indians in westerns could be so

inhumanly atrocious to nice innocent

family farmers. As time went on, I

realized all history is spun like that.

We are still too much acting as if we had a right to use all of nature we can muster. This attitude has somewhat abated regarding humans. However, we are reaching a critical point where nature has no recovery space left to balance our egomania, which turns its continued destruction into ours.

we create needlessly harsh conditions that we then fight in endless battles

Surfing is an allegory of life with less hostile animals in the water.

IV. REALIZATION

most of us go out of our way
to continue on beaten paths

Many ads sell dishonesties of being
able to reach depicted unattainable
ideal states by way of the advertised
collateral product or service.

my girl always stays my girl
no matter her condition or age
her smile makes me uncurl
from any sadness rage or frown
even when it was her
who wound me up or down

don't take guff from anyone
times it's rough but must be done
not to become routinely scuffed

you first must secure
an endangered light
to carefully then fan its flame

cannon fodder we easily scare
they own the rudder saying they care
we pull the ores and swallow waves
told free to leave yet we remain slaves
all to buy furnishings houses or cars
afford vacations restaurants bars

IV. REALIZATION

gamekeepers we notice

may mimic to be

natural parts of our territory

already know but refuse to see

we made a go of life just to be

took to advice not to turn the key

now we co-own the conspiracy

put on the spot embarrassed or seized

ignorant of who has catered our feast

or who's thrown our scraps and dies

we feign surprise to just realize

when all along we averted our eyes

our only true shot
at lasting survival
is passing on
traditions of love

she claims not to know anymore
the more she's compelled to find out
covers windows and locks the door
but it is her insides that shout

The secret to securing power is
rendering subjects concerned about
losing rights, privileges, or property
and appearing to be their patron.

IV. REALIZATION

i only like real
if it matches my dreams
move to repeal
if it threatens their seams

Hierarchy refutes human dignity
expressed in harmonic needs. Peace
cannot occur or endure until it ends.

we've been kept blind
but taught that we see
fearful to find
what life would be
if we knew all withheld

some people hold back
because living their truth
threatens to burn them or others
so they keep track
act mostly couth
whereupon nobody bothers

genius is often troubled and unclear
thus it can be seen with folly as a peer

people who deem untruths fair means
for convincing others of truth
continue the very process
by which they arrived at theirs

V.
ASPIRATION

V. ASPIRATION

Beethoven to housekeeper:
I've composed a symphony that
redefines music.
How does it go?
Dadadadaaah, dadadadaaah!
That's really nice, Maestro.

he swore i will surprise you one day
like springtime green
on a long deemed dead tree

her presence
makes me luxuriate
in necessities of life

called listlessness his age's top effect
steadily rising through his existence
never rivalled by a wish to redirect

she was their mother daughter wife
now there's none left to leave her
still is she free to begin a new life

grandma said
it's the little things
that make or break your day
so when i feel bad
or affairs are jinxed
i search the clouds for a ray

V. ASPIRATION

talking to you

who isn't yet born

version of me

rising with the new morn

will you set out

to make things better

or fight again

to not get more forlorn

hop along

be true and humble

times you stumble or skip a beat

you're often wrong

or when right you fumble

so don't grumble life is not neat

but best led by song and on our feet

poetry has us collecting our hints
bells in hope of being rung

people get old
when they stop making friends

first order efforts
should be to stop
sabotaging ourselves

holding our own ambitions in prison
we slip others unknowing the key

V. ASPIRATION

asked for advice

to my former form

i would withhold

so as not to conform

my tired expectations

looking around

why can't we still fathom

this isn't at all about us

climbing alone

without a peer

feels like a tone

nobody can hear

reaching the top

without the climb

feels like a flop

and much like a crime

the world is too full

of those because

and not enough

of in spites

i thought i felt i had the impression

most sorries start like that

time to come off our tired horses

walk the rest of the way instead

V. ASPIRATION

girl i met in paris

the problem with her care is

she knows me better

than my own kind

it's making her talk

like an angry mother

would have preferred her

to be something other

she's not what i hoped to find

owe her a letter

while my eyes get wetter

why i had to walk

leaving her behind

we earn elevation

after learning to be humble

i read she finally got her premiere
all to a tee
seems she conquered her fear
not being good enough

mask me
unmask me
that is what passion
makes you do

some may be crushed
by the paths we take
most damage hushed
too much is at stake

V. ASPIRATION

she liked blooms

that thrive in winter

all its glooms

vexed by their bright splinter

cannot retain a sure footing

i have not played this guitar for ages

quietly kept my scars and rages

someday i'll find new strings

her ostentatious lack of motion

gives him painful pause

maybe she's foreign to the notion

that all he does deserves applause

he was romantic

girls matter of fact

deemed it a tactic

for courage he lacked

asking them what they wanted

hold me

don't tap me out

on my back

though it's well known

that life and love are dear

humans are prone

betraying this idea

V. ASPIRATION

every time we think we're too good
a little angel stubs its foot
and curses us to hell

she ran out of stories
that didn't repeat
but not out of worries
about her feet
carrying her beyond

the clueless and those of depravity
and others who won't dare trying
worsen this planet's gravity
but cannot keep us from flying

Communities in which people of the
same or a similar mind can live freer
according to their shared intentions
have the potential of reducing friction
and increasing positive experiences.

cadence enhances
her parent's bourgeois trances
hates what she is hearing
runs out of patience
for wasted chances
for being told she's less endearing
for being reminded she's living in sin
she is committed to do her own thing
uncaring if her ice turns thin
from the fire that burns within

V. ASPIRATION

you are too much
in love with yourself
to need the love of others

thrown in the water
i got pinned down
fighting the tow
in fear i would drown
not visualizing floating free

i cannot wait
to hear the music
that must be playing
inside you

one main lesson learned last year

never again move a nightstand

with a drawer without drawers

.

err on the side of love

and you will never be wrong

you keep carping people are like rats

i say one day they might have to be

she says i am too content

being with her

V. ASPIRATION

trusting wolves' instincts
to take her home
when all they can think of
is homing in on her

The real problem with positive
conditioning is not finding or
recalling the how but the why.

squirrels don't leap
without knowing their landing
still they go fast
without first demanding
branches in the right spot

if you had a choice
to be remembered
have a voice
after you're dismembered
would you want recordings of tone
videos photos words cut in stone
or live on in souls of the living
for all you have been giving

He: "I wonder why soap operas aren't available for streaming from when they first began."
She: "Probably because it would take a lifetime to watch. [pause]. I think that could be something nice to do for us in the afterlife."

V. ASPIRATION

everyone else loves rainbows
he's more absorbed
by the half that's underground

is life's ultimate purpose
to take all in and get all out
grow satisfied and wise from this
to one day be calm and recollected

you merely like me
but do not love me
so i get lost
don't want to be found
turning fox to your lovely hound

Finding who we are is a second step. We first must know how to achieve that. We must then decide whether we wish to remain true to the state we find or change it. In this process, we must imagine changed versions of us. Finally, we must comprehend how to go about securing these objectives.

break or break out
shut up or shout
hold it in or let it out
is what our struggle is all about
yet lose or win
we sign back in
ready for another bout

V. ASPIRATION

if i woke and knew
the world was not true
would i jump upset out of bed
or go back to sleeping instead
or would i think of what to do
to ban these chimeras from my head

when patience wears out
like holes joining in socks
frustration roars loud
like a race car on blocks
nerves scratch on slate
we're convinced it's too late
all these are signs of new beginnings
turning harsh lessons into winnings
paving paths that will never run out

we all fail our aspirations

some make it worse

by giving them up

i had a vision at rising sun

that we were two

and still remained one

let's not let us become offended

our bearing be known

by its gears upended

or swaddled cuddled

everything muddled

with endless supplies of band-aid

VI.
PERSISTENCE

VI. PERSISTENCE

old and new ways of showing love
are necessary to keep it alive

coming back has little karma
if one did not leave before
but you and i don't need this drama
to understand we are joined evermore

life as myth
as he arranged his
going out
and into fashion
he never changes
just living his passion

i still stand

despite of it all

calm command

at the height of a squall

unafraid of resistance

fighting the certainties

in our lives

rather than growing around them

once we internalize

time is precious

nothing again

can put us at ease

VI. PERSISTENCE

blooming for bees
in the midst of winter
scorning the freeze
she is a sprinter
gracefully resting
the year at peace

sincerely promised her
to be a better man
like he could shed his fur
not grow it back again

if you became a parchment leaf
you'd still be pristine green to me

the devil whispered

there's nobody out there

yes screamed many nobodies

doggedly misbehave

haughty or akin

with indignant hints

we're to hide our grin

at the delusion

they hatched themselves in

her love is not earned

and it cannot be burned

life's evils fight this solemn constant

VI. PERSISTENCE

she is the morning

he is the dark

they shortly meet

and then must part

still they are married forever

ever since

their hearts got cold

they could not be consoled

he always commits

to live tomorrow

distraction won't quit

to his compounding sorrow

i'll be as free as you desire
i'll cherish thee until i expire
all the world's pee
can't extinguish my fire

when you are lost
by yourself or others
find a new post
act like nothing much bothers
and in the long run it won't

keep going
she said
as he walked beside her

VI. PERSISTENCE

i often go back to the wishing tree

because my leaves

are completely free

she won't force me to stay planted

you leave much to be desired

just a touch

and i stop feeling mired

i hope i'll never get enough

those once abused

have become the abusers

righteous and proud

so much evil to shroud

i feel the soft sand
as i clench my hand
reinforcing its escape

and so i ask before rooting my tree
will you forever come for me
will you at some time count the cost
when i grate you or you see me lost
will you eventually betray
hating i drew you into my fray

i will court you as if a knight
i will support you in taking flight
even if you won't return to me

VI. PERSISTENCE

give me your worst
it won't sate my thirst
for i am cursed
by love punishing me

hundred years later
new blood
to revive him
still his mind
stays stuck in the past

mistaking change for running away
opens the range for ills to stay
or roam with us wherever we may

i'd lay down my life
to lie by your side
peace or strife
my love will not hide

bash my head
out of what i said
we both may try
but we'll never forget

putting new tires
on burned motorcycles
and we still wonder
we're getting nowhere

VI. PERSISTENCE

when i'm not with you
you're most with me

women can make a man
or destroy him
once he's entangled in their charms
that's why i ran
and tried to avoid them
still i am longing to be in their arms
no matter what i do to be free
nothing about them will let me be

now's more important
than being remembered

set for eternity waiting all life

honesty makes people gag
they carry conscience in a bag
not adding to where it might tear
their ideals fade from idle wear

most think you are wavering
not waving anybody's flag

you and you and you again
always newfangled and yet familiar

VI. PERSISTENCE

you keep me on my feet
and wanting to lie down

climbing the ladder into love's heaven
takes two tied hearts for every rung

am i here
when she does not acknowledge me
i would not want it any different

she says she won't leave
and he must stop waiting

you don't write me
still i am written
no need to fight me
i'm already smitten
hoping you find me
somewhere in your sight

years for her
to tell she loved him
many more in a fight to forget

all his paths went out of his way
looking for her
against staggering odds

VI. PERSISTENCE

embraces him with essence and being
forming a sheltering mantle of love
open defenseless trusting inside

goldfish circling
his glass clad bowl
silently mouthing
wherareyou
wherareyou

she lets him loose
on her to devour
cannot choose
to not want his power

he told me each time
you need to go
before they won't let you leave
you must cut the line
of the boat you row
though you'll be called a thief
your freedom is lonely
and compromised only
to give your heartache reprieve

Most won't change directions since they imagine a destination that makes up for their discomfort - until they get there. Then they stick with the destination because they wasted all this time and energy getting there.

VI. PERSISTENCE

without breaking

hearts have no facets

turning dull white

into rainbows of light

stay when it feels

you have arrived

your travels continue anyway

petals of blooms

bring forth a crown

that one time rested in its seed

before they arrest into a dry frown

their core returning to this creed

every time calamity strikes
likes of cowards say they'll pray
knights attend and won't turn away

we see what we want to see
try to portray it reality
are we blind or just resolute dreamers

she's the prize i'll never win
fault her eyes for the shape i'm in
wishing one day they'd shine on me
tell me lies that this love's a sin
every cell cries but she won't give in
there is simply no lock for my key

VI. PERSISTENCE

The universe moves by laws we only begin to understand. Our experience is that we come from and go to the infinite, making us wonder how and why we're here as if we could affect it.

Why do many of the highly revered philosophical concepts the "Old Greeks" coined sound like something my grandma could have thought of? Like the Brothers Grimm, they were largely collectors and purveyors of accumulated lore. Most consists of traditional cultural concepts, myths, and common sense, conventional wisdom, or naïve, mistaken science.

music was killed
by staccato slurs
only angry remains

told some days he'd like to travel
but they never seemed to listen

puppeteers can claim success again
we are on board with the evil insane
common sense widely is being let go
someone far away we do not know
strangely determined to be our foe
when each time now as it was then
we picked the fight by pushing them

VI. PERSISTENCE

their love describes
as an endless first kiss
he won't leave her side
and she never his

she learned to admire this ugly crab
though always jilting him like a scab
he still maintained his uplifting swag
with unaffected entangling charm

ridicule and berating
best attempts curbing their drive
underestimating
this makes them fight for their life

some of us will not stand up for love
since it floored them before

we often falsely justify or over-glorify
that what we want must be done
but just like
we can't blind or shine on the sun
souls are unforgiving

he thought i'll be sorry i left
but she wants to be alone
maybe my absence
will make her bereft
and she'll ask me to come home

VII.
HAPPENSTANCE

VII. HAPPENSTANCE

maybe you are correct
we will someday be done
but it is not over yet
between beckons all this fun
that might set the future in our debt

each crisis divides
the grate- mind- and helpful
from users and complainers

why would i tell you
'bout loves i lost
till getting to you
the love of which i'm found

i've given up

on my life to rhyme

sequences falling in place

or forcing their fit

so i can in time

die after winning the race

sometimes she had to

give herself up

floating serendipity

her language

very different from mine

but what we speak akin

VII. HAPPENSTANCE

the northern girl seems not so tough
says meet me at sunset in the bluff
he cannot help but heartily laugh
covertly hoping her spelling is off
and she does not think him immature

missing miracles is ungrateful
but so is hoping for them

morning at the hardware store
he asked a checkout girl
are you free
yes and no said she
proof of living philosophy

the problem is

we have to take sides

because we have to

stop the worst fools

when we find one

who takes our crap

and won't be gone

when we're lazy and fat

might as well call it love

she plays with me

should i be honored

can't ask her for the rules

VII. HAPPENSTANCE

when good luck ends and turns
good luck friends not often
are ones that you can count on
but strangers' hearts will soften
and help move your mountain
soothing first and second grade burns

if i were a god i would be saying
i got no envoys you should be paying
gave you enough to stop the praying
stand on your feet and i'd also resent
you think you go free if you repent
that i have a childish need for praise
and if i don't get it i'd cause malaise
expect less talk instead more good act
adept respect for my nature intact

love a woman who wants me around
without particular thought of purpose
am i just lucky or is my fate bound
to this bright star
that renders me wordless

if you would tell me i am no good
if you'd fell me like overgrown wood
you would not hear a plea
just where i stood

she plays games
not thinking of winning
but to lose herself in them

VII. HAPPENSTANCE

why do most logical ways of being
somehow remain a dream

When the discovery of a pink dwarf
planet hundred and fifty times farther
out from the Sun than Earth sounds
for a change like really good news . . .

half a teen nary
i tried to imagine
the girl i would marry
this came down crashing
she's nothing like you
an inconceivable dream come true

am i stupid to fall for her graces
the wryest smile
and i cannot tie laces
i am unfit to follow her paces
by more than a mile
but she's taking me places
i'd like to stay for a while

one of the hardest ways to be
is longing for you for sure
once i thought you belong to me
now you say that is no more
still there's a shimmer of light i see
a cure we may find for this malady
scaring you to the core
that i will treat you like i did before

VII. HAPPENSTANCE

her heart's like a bank
in granting him credit
he leaves his check blank
even after she said it

what if i were
her everything
i could not bear
the fix i'd be in

justify misdeeds
by failures of others
so you don't have to
address your own

i had a dream of her
loving me
but if she were
i could not see
love must progress in phases

is it coincidence
ears are made for both
hearing and equilibrium

twelve hundred million paces
from a custard pearl
girls coincide their phases
tracing its gravity's whirl

VII. HAPPENSTANCE

whatever my course
my love makes me come back
or is it yours
keeping my heart on track

she doesn't know herself anymore
how a smart elf could turn to a bore
maybe her wits just were aging

why was i thinking
you too could not sleep
don't even know you
why feels this so deep
let's talk about this tomorrow

you make me mad and drive me crazy
why i fell so bad is sometimes hazy
i guess i like a good fog

she's sure we are bound
for a special connection
since our cars bumped
in the intersection

he was the fool who fell for your spice
without you skipping in stride
you picked him up
threw him into your stew
and took him for a mild ride

VII. HAPPENSTANCE

we're dialed on high
scoping following trends
purchase our dreams
and think of stars as friends
when people cry we blur our lens
accept the lie no one repents
but secretly we all look to the sky
pray it all ends so we might try
a new life making sense

The purpose of poetry, written or read alike, seems different at times. Some use it as means to express searching, give life to wishes, brag about what they have got or found, or bemoan the despair of failure.

no reason apparent

why they should meet

and still they felt

it was meant to happen

Sincere people are afraid of a their apparent counterpart because they are bound for ultimate surrender. Despite all investigations, it takes a lot of courage and trust for each to hand over the keys to their fortress.

we could have missed each other

instead are now missing each other

VIII.
MOMENTS

VIII. MOMENTS

we all know that a moment will come
when all other moments will have run

you turn and pierce me
with blue-rayed skewers
raising your glass
toasting this is to us

drudging curmudgeon
when woken up
she sits him down
with a steaming cup
turning up his dreary frown
so he can work as a happy clown

what i recall

are little gestures

fleeting markers

arresting my heart

smell roses

even at the cost of bleeding

can you just be

with your head in the sun

nothing to see

about what can be done

nothing lost and nothing won

undefined furloughs from time

VIII. MOMENTS

falling in love is meant to be
on a moment's notice
followed by periods
of accommodation

he made his decisions
by drop of a hat
to counter derisions
or win a bet

i love her dance
when she picks up clothes
into her hands
with curled-around toes

she says things such

i like biting your teeth

or love you so much

i forget to breathe

none of my poems can match her

the car was drifting

our bodies lifting

for a short moment

we felt no weight

the space where you breathe

was a vacuum before

with insufficient suction

VIII. MOMENTS

i met this stranger
who put me to shame
asking his function
before his name
like he was just a pawn in the game

after all time
i still learn to exist
in the momentum of her kiss

she was mine
for only a moment
and that is enough
since there's no forever

the model said she did not eat
still giving heed to a basic need
and quickly was consumed

my deficit of attention
is in equal parts due to a penchant
of wanting to live every moment and
sidestep torment that might foment

tiny street angel
hugging my leg
melting my heart
to do my part
so your mother won't have to beg

VIII. MOMENTS

new as if he had not lived already

he took the wheel
and made her squeal
the shape of drives to come

beaten again
to all my intentions
bat of her eyes
i lose the script
she owns the dote
against any preventions
shall i give in
live on scales always tipped

i recall the tow when love was new
thus making it so a moment or two
heart muscle memory

after all they said has been done
they do one more dance
before they are gone
soft with respect
and cheeks barely touching

you'll be the one
i think of when i die
not by the ways that love goes on
but how you killed me with your lie

VIII. MOMENTS

you say you could love me
don't know yet quite how
sipping dry chablis
we drift in the now

we are here only blinks of god's eye
hope she sees us before our good bye
are we just fillers or universe pillars
or do we even care or try

this breaks my stride
and makes me pause
think bricks of life
and poetic visions

a wink of your eye
gives a flutter to my heart

what more can i tell
you don't already know
by our eyes' fleeting meeting
and nervously looking away
where did my courage go
why is my mind so slow
i fear my heart will stop beating
if you did not find a reason to stay

once in a while some truth pops up
quickly pulled under in seas of lies

VIII. MOMENTS

chance glanced eyes on malibu beach
she a girl who had kept out of reach
starved by her rise
she dropped her guise
asked what i was reading

walking malibu beach again
i saw she had come to cry
loathing to spy i stayed when asked
but tried to console her in vain
she was dying from endless lying
from living behind a mask
all i suggested eluded her grasp
so i told her tales of weightless flying
breathing dancing and being free
after surmounting odds valiantly
listening close she sat deeply sighing
pouring her heart out into the sea

she says "you're sappy"

when i'm half unhappy

she spends her preciousness with me

are we fighting or playing

poetry is the language of dreams

touching tips of our waking mind

during split seconds

of switching defenses

the little boy inside appeared

VIII. MOMENTS

a moment's blink
is already tragic
don't want to grieve
the beauty i missed

pausing passions
makes you lose their thread

she knew not this night's
mysterious loner
by his heart nor mind nor deed
just listening to his lore of knights
seeking honor fighting for rights
and tending to the weak

just for a moment
she thought to reply
barring fear's foment
that she was shy

time we collect all our life
spilled in derelict moments

before i asked you already forgave
i'll keep this beautiful sentiment safe

a lifetime's blink in eternity's eye

IX.
GRACE

IX. GRACE

she cut moon and stars
from her paper heart
and pictures of him
going back to the start
till macramé beauty emerged

you my sweet
are proving true
i can keep cake
and eat it too

the pacing of the world is off
binge everything
still not enough

you broke down all my fences
still made the intrusion feel right
robbed me of most of my senses
dipped me in fragrant warm light

lately romps in which i took joy
seem distractions waiting for you
what a man wants is not a toy
true satisfaction is from being true

the world is divided
in rapers and healers
self-conscious innocence
passes them both

IX. GRACE

i cannot fathom
how love at first sight
can be intuitively right
and i play catch up
with my synapses

you're looking cute
like a forlorn puppy
though i'm a brute
in your hands i'm putty
good we're not scoring who won

she holds me dear
like i'm worth the effort

a bodice aids this voluptuous goddess
making a man just let all else be
some of her rivals call her immodest
she sees no reason she should not be

when leaving her
for only the day
makes heart strings stir
and while you're away
the duet keeps on playing

my love is special
she makes me love girls
simply by type association

IX. GRACE

like the newt maimed
that grew back an arm
pain became moot
and i'm over the harm
you crushed my heart
when you left me

disdain for folks from other countries
vanishes quickly when we're in theirs
lost hurt but finding somebody cares

today she placed curved index fingers
perking up from the sides of her head
as if she could ever bug me in bed

you wouldn't put paint
on a flower or pearl
why then place it upon a girl

in a few years all tears will have dried
rage or shame of lost chances subside
all our tangibles stripped off the bone
nothingness save for few cuts in stone
as long as someone pays for our tomb

she searches fights for jabs she missed
ruminating she should have said this
but it wouldn't have moved any lines
only compounded her lack of bliss

IX. GRACE

don't need to fight
to prove i'm a man
don't need a thing
to show who i am
all i need is to always be true
lucky that you want this too

we need to stall telling anyone
we cannot exist without them
until we have made them
feel this way as well

you're beautiful in so many ways
it's almost unfair to the others

i tell her proudly
my poems are about her
she does not care
because she is the source

Why do so many artists suffer from exhaustion, drug abuse, and mental problems? Apart from the strain to become or remain relevant, this is because art requires opening yourself up - and many get hurt that way.

Names were invented so people don't identify us by how we impress them.

IX. GRACE

god if he exists

and consciously created us

loves his work but does not need us

no need to tell him how great he is

he'd already know or have doubts

because he would worry about us

an obvious blemish on his record

would want us to be great as well

help one another and not compete

would loathe us for quarrels generally

and particularly about which of us

talks and wails best to or fights for

imaginary parents friends or demons

having everything and nothing

leaves us two ways without care

don't get me wrong i'm looking at you
but if i came on i could not do
what you so richly deserve
not really sorry i don't have the nerve
letting her down and dishonoring you

no matter you are
i take your hand
no matter how far
with you i stand
no one should be without caring

doubts if we liked or loved each other
naturally never occurred

IX. GRACE

behold a flower be one with it
play guitar resonate with it
love this woman then breathe a bit
sense the world in full color

if you need reasons to have lots of fun
love reminiscence and circumstance
all grow into myths in the longer run
this is why we can't shun any chance
to shed our skins and shine in the sun
jest embrace sing laugh and dance

love only works
not joined at the hip

solitude but not alone
because i'm with you
which makes it home

the places i touch you
no one else permitted
why is it me
you want so deep in your soul

down by the irrigation ditch
she lives with her imagination rich
a careless pretty little light flower
while envy and salaciousness cower
snakes calling her spinelessly a witch

IX. GRACE

don't bother if you want true truth
with messes in which humans behave
listen to subtle music soothe
look at the glistening of a wave

i don't know how it used to be
that what i needed i could not see
all it took was to finally listen
what heart and mind screamed
they were missing

she does not like for him to curse
given a drink she will be its nurse
loves cold nights in long nightgowns

after alone it's finally you
who quenches my heart
while stoking its fire
could it be true
it was you from the start
unknown now known
proving fate a liar

though it may fade
from an effortless stride
beauty is made
to destroy foolish pride
moving the stayed
and shining love's light
baring vanity's desperate plight
to dress up ugliness with a parade

IX. GRACE

We only can fool our minds, but we cannot make up our hearts. They are our true compass, good or bad.

used to be easier even in troubles
taking time out to feel or think
sitting down with a meal or drink
get some air talk listen and repair
edge out joy from disaster's brink
reel back a sea of causes for despair

nobody cares
that
nobody cares

you know why i love her
she speaks to the stars
the same she addresses
a homeless person

what happened to just being
instead of advertising
what happened to just saying
instead of aggrandizing
what happened to just loving
instead of continually pricing

she once was a whispering opine
now she yells unvarnished pains

IX. GRACE

their bodies' language
stays mostly apart
and still they have
full understanding

he's corny
loves kitsch
and talks in clichés
but has most survey
in this mired maze

apple plum and pear
bathe in ice cream air
fall is suggesting a dare

i asked to keep a wild baby hare
father said no it would never submit
even if one took good care of it
as things now proceed
i would wish when i split
i could be reborn
that untamed and deep

the tell of love is resonance

often it's not those with all the words
who are the most profound
wisdom takes listening to the birds
silence can be the most sound

IX. GRACE

Problems arise because we over-
estimate or underestimate. The way
to avoid this is to be calm, careful,
and methodical, and to not prejudge.
This precludes disappointment.

she could turn him on forever
or turn on this man and sever
freedoms from not being in love

old lady applauds them is good folk
you criticize her grammar and diction
serving your vain superiority fiction
like a pig scratching itself on an oak

all are worthy

of our attention

if it is loving

and unassuming

how do you love

eight nine ten billion people

start with one

and work yourself up

she kept enticing

come with me

where

the fool kept inquiring

IX. GRACE

Is a simple belief in good and in luck
naively wrong or is it empirical truth?

though i don't dance
any woman who tangoes
has my temper with her on its feet

you had my love just showing up
there's nothing more to be earned

he tends to scold incompatible moods
she puts on only well-fitting boots

We must first find or define a box to
make sure our thoughts are outside of
it. And having gained perspective, our
concerns remain focused on the box.

if we announced our unmet desires
trouncing all gossip and judgment
and moved ahead from then on free
we might build genuine harmony

nothing love makes her do
ever seems dirty
she knows that this is
how flowers are made

IX. GRACE

We do not need affirmation and
become immune to false judgment
when we understand to be and
become harmonious within our self.

life seeks to expand
bursting at the seams
will not be contained
we can learn in reams

one cannot love
without breaking down
to fragments
that make up the essence of stars

it's really simple we complicate life
to get away with clear infractions

inflections of your head neck spine
make me believe it might be time
i trade in my poetry for our rhyme

you tell me much in your breathing
that's how spirits speak

eighty-eight keys to find to her heart
he plays around but she wants a dart

IX. GRACE

tender words repeatedly spoken
gradually parted her lips
this was merely an opening token
to machinations of her hips

We may not always know when people are in need of receiving an encouraging word. But we can always be certain it will elevate their mood.

lasting desire
is unfulfilled
since we soon tire
when tension is killed

When you sense animosity, reserve,
or fear in others, step forward with an
out-reaching hand, look them in the
eyes and say: I want to be your friend.

seeing him breaks a spell of years
visions she conjured
through veils of tears
scattered now by waking

love talk make music write
hear your self think
your life is not yet set in ink
try and you might die tickled pink

X.
ROOM TO PLY

X. ROOM TO PLY

ROOM TO PLY spans lovers' emotions and motions while they are courting and after eventually perceiving they want to share their life with the other.

To give love and be loved to the greatest degree, they want so much to be united and are ready to give up all by which they do not fit together. Until they find they lose themselves in this mode, and will ultimately lose each other. Being one is impossible and the notion denies the essence and dynamics of love, which are outgoing.

Solving this conundrum is the key to every lasting relationship. ROOM TO PLY offers perspective and courage that it is possible if lovers give each other room to ply – meaning space to unfold at a risk of not neatly matching.

i was alone
so i would roam
the countryside
without a home

when i saw you
your spirit shone
conquered my pride
my heart was blown

had not been ready
for going too steady
but you were so heady
i wrote you a poem

X. ROOM TO PLY

you were uptight

yet that was alright

cause you were polite

and threw me a bone

met up in company

soon it was plain to see

that you were into me

matching our tone

then i was lost without you

will you make my dreams come true

i don't know what's real

anymore

please give me your love

you're what i've been dreaming of

i will give you in return my life

and more

entered your world

first on the phone

talking all night

into the unknown

i tried to please

almost a clone

tailored my flight

for seams to be sown

X. ROOM TO PLY

you would ignite
and we did unite
within a fortnight
i made you moan

then i was all lost in you
we were one no longer two
i don't know who i'm without you
anymore

i am so in love
and we fit like hand in glove
i don't know where you and i end
anymore

but our minds
had ways of their own
everyday rites
set them in stone

turned out our lives
were only on loan
and we would fight
to get back our zone

i played your knight
veiling my fright
feigning delight
against my poor heart's blight

X. ROOM TO PLY

you say you have no life
and all this compromise
makes you lose sight of
the person you are

i know that feeling well
curbing me casts a spell
and endless arguments
turn into war

our embraces
have become shackles
no humor traces
left in our heckles

both pacing frantically
in our cages
i want out you want out
hopelessness rages

then i was lost still with you
i put all my trust in you
now you tell me you don't love me
anymore

how did we go wrong
our love was just like a song
but all harmonies we made
have ended long

we are undone is our flame gone
no one was right nobody won

drained of all fun
i lost my sun
banned from the bright
dark without dawn

i'm sitting in my basement's shadow
never have been near as sad oh
why have things turned out so bad
all offenses that we bellowed
and the others that we swallowed
left me much more matte than mad

locked myself into my hell oh
all my heart strings sound like cello
being played by saws and cruelly cut
rain or sunshine it won't go away
night or daytime it won't go away
always wanted love in me to stay
now it's leading fast to my decay

doesn't matter what i lose or find
you are in the center of my mind
doesn't matter if your mean or kind
without you life is an endless grind
wish i had not left our chance behind
must be true that love is really blind
i know we both felt we were confined
still i sense our souls closely entwined

so i am wondering what to do
i don't think i have a clue
will i ever know true love anymore
i'm no good alone
or with someone i have shown
thought who i was was enough
but that's no more

is there a chance
for us to atone
cut though the fence
admit not disown
from ashes glow
are we able to grow
learn to live right
and not put on a show

can we despite

our pain invite

instead of indict

develop insight

and you say i am still afraid

and don't want to rush our fate

i don't know

what our future has in store

it is getting late

we should simply go to bed

let a new day bring

some answers to our door

X. ROOM TO PLY

morning's coming cold and grey
yesterday we thought you'd stay
now i see
your things are all but packed

courage fallen by the way
fearing there's more hell to pay
we both know
our odds are highly stacked

there are many reasons why
we can make each other cry
we're so different
and our nerves are frayed

but down deep there is no lie
this is why we've got to try
turn this love around before too late

and you say too
i still love you
but i cannot wait in queue
until we see eye to eye
anymore

i am here for you
but my life's no longer true
if you won't let me be me
anymore

X. ROOM TO PLY

i will wait for you forever
though forever's never true
some hearts move on like the weather
i will not get over you

still some cords are left to sever
will pride play us as a fool
do we think of us too clever
or do we go back to school

i want things to get much better
you're not one i want to lose
but our strings may slowly fetter
choking us into a noose

i will not be closely tethered
and i won't walk in your shoes
i have gotten tarred and feathered
thinking all i want is you

all we know
and where we go
all we need
and all we bleed

all we crave
and misbehave
all we hope
pretend to cope

X. ROOM TO PLY

all we dare
and all we care
all we find
or leave behind

all we give
and all we live
all we lose
divide in twos

all we lie and all we die
all this bakes or takes our pie
all this makes us low or high
all this braids or breaks our tie

i you

us two

wrong true

black and white or hue

regret about what needs to be said

swimming dry or wet

foe and yet

each other's pet

still life is humdrum

if you cannot run

and come back home

after you're done

X. ROOM TO PLY

we reunite

without overwrite

will be forthright

so we won't shun

just realize

we cannot own

each other's light

as we're searching on

we can stay two

without dread or feeling blue

if we just support each other

in our core

finding out with you
we can make our dreams come true
since we've come to know us deeper
so much more

we can only fly
if we leave us room to ply
but i'd like to travel with you
evermore

again you and me
guess now we'll see
how life will be
while we are free

www.ingramcontent.com/pod-product-compliance
Lightning Source LLC
Chambersburg PA
CBHW032109090426
42743CB00007B/288